Recorder
from the Beginning

Book 1

John Pitts

Published by
EJA Publications
14-15 Berners Street, London W1T 3LJ, UK.

Exclusive Distributors:

Music Sales Limited
Distribution Centre, Newmarket Road, Bury St Edmunds,
Suffolk, IP33 3YB, UK.

Music Sales Corporation
257 Park Avenue South, New York, NY 10010, USA.

Music Sales Pty Limited
20 Resolution Drive, Caringbah, NSW 2229, Australia.

Acknowledgements

The publishers would like to thank the following for permission to include copyright material:

'Tadpoles' (Fyleman) reproduced by kind permission of the Society of Authors as the literary
representatives of the Estate of Rose Fyleman. All Rights Reserved.

'Traffic Jam' (Holdstock) reproduced by kind permission of Jan Holdstock. All Rights Reserved.

Illustrations by Tom Wanless.

Design by Butterworth Design.

Music processing and layout by Camden Music.

This recorder course in three stages has be[en] [... for children aged]
7 upwards. Since publication it has beco[me one of the most popular]
schemes used in many parts of the world.

Recorder from the Beginning assumes no previous knowledge of either
music or the recorder, and full explanations are provided at every stage so
that specialist teaching is not essential. Teacher's Books are available for
each stage, and these contain simple piano accompaniments, guitar chord
symbols and suggestions for each tune, often using pitched/unpitched
percussion.

All three Pupil's Books are also available in Book & CD editions (CDs not
available separately) and the recorded accompaniments will enhance
any level of practice or performance, whether by beginners or advanced
players. They include a model version of each tune (except in Book 3),
followed by exciting, stylish accompaniments for recorders to play along
with, both in school and at home.

Revision of the original books for the new full-colour edition has allowed
me to make various changes to improve the scheme. The eight extra pages
in Book 1 have allowed for some new tunes and rounds, whilst retaining
the well-known favourites that have helped to make the scheme such an
enduring success. Book 2 has 13 new items as well as new optional duets.
Book 3 has the most changes of all, to allow for the introduction of 27
new pieces. I have also made a small change to the order of introducing
new notes.

For all these changes in the different books we have recorded exciting
new accompaniment tracks for the CDs, plus improved tracks for some of
the previous pieces. I have also strengthened and increased the optional
opportunities for recorder players to contribute to music units in the
National Curriculum, by combining their recorder playing with class music
activities such as singing and the use of pitched and unpitched
percussion.

I know you will enjoy the lovely pictures created by Tom Wanless, and I
wish to thank Tom for his stunning contribution. I also wish to thank my
wife Maureen for her never-ending support, help and encouragement over
all the years.

I hope the revised edition will be enjoyed as much as the earlier version,
and that you will soon have new favourites to add to your present ones.

John Pitts 2004

Contents

Acknowledgements

The publishers would like to thank the following for permission to use their copyright material:

"Tadpoles" (Fyleman) Reproduced by kind permission of The Society of Authors as the Literary Representatives of the Estate of Rose Fyleman. All rights reserved. "Traffic Jam" words by Jan Holdstock.

Holding your recorder

Hold your recorder in front of you.
Put your left hand near the top.
Put your right hand near the bottom.

Press your left thumb over the hole underneath the recorder.
Cover the top hole nearest your mouth with your first finger.

Put your right thumb under the recorder opposite the fourth hole.
This helps to hold the recorder.
Look at the picture to help you.

Do not move your fingers.
Now you are ready to play your first note.

Beginning to play

Put the tip of your recorder between your lips.
Do not let it touch your teeth.

Blow gently into the recorder by saying "tu".
It should make a sound called **note B**.

Play note B several times.
Remember to say "tu" each time you play the note.
This is called **tonguing**.

Be careful. Only your left thumb and first finger should cover any holes.

Note B

Hold your recorder like you did before.
Only your left thumb and first finger should cover holes.

Play note B four times.
Remember to say "tu" each time.
Make each note sound for the same time.

tu tu tu tu

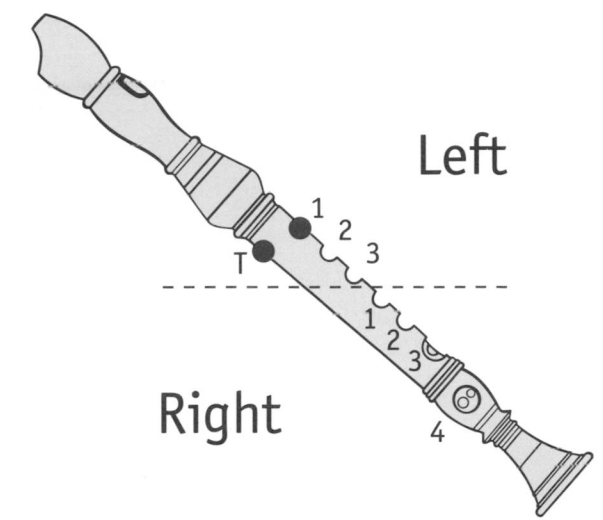

Left

Right

Diagrams like the one on the right show the fingering for each note.
A magenta circle shows that you should cover this hole.

We write musical notes on a set of
5 lines called a **stave**.
Here is note B written four times
on the stave.

tu   tu   tu   tu

The sign 𝄞 at the beginning of each stave is called a **treble clef**.

Play note B again four times.
Check your fingers are in the right place.

note B
B
Left
1
2
3
T
1
2
3
4
Right

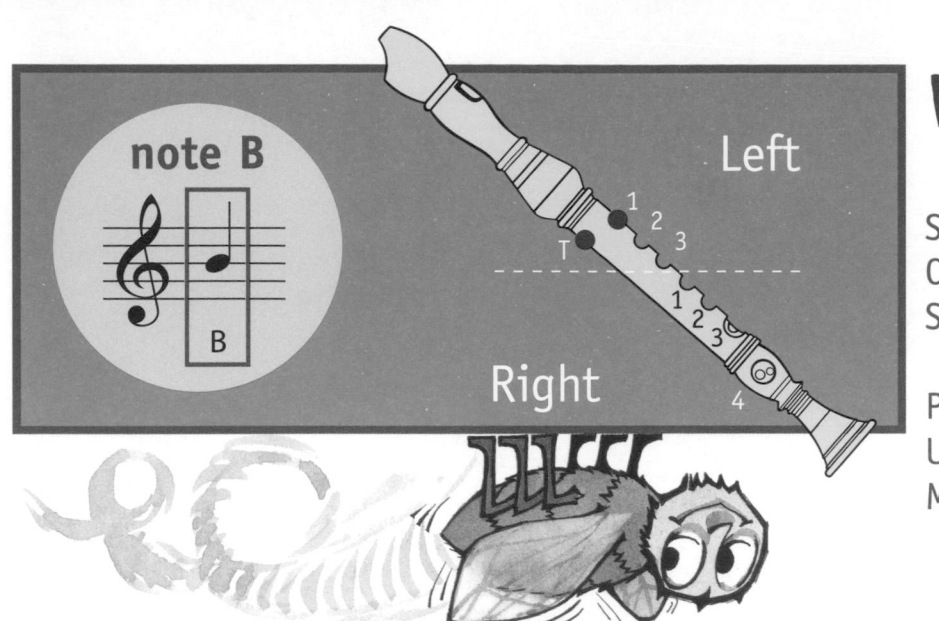

Little Fly

Say the words to this song.
Clap in time with the words as you say them.
See how some words last longer then others.

Play the tune on your recorder.
Use note B.
Make the notes match the pattern of the words.

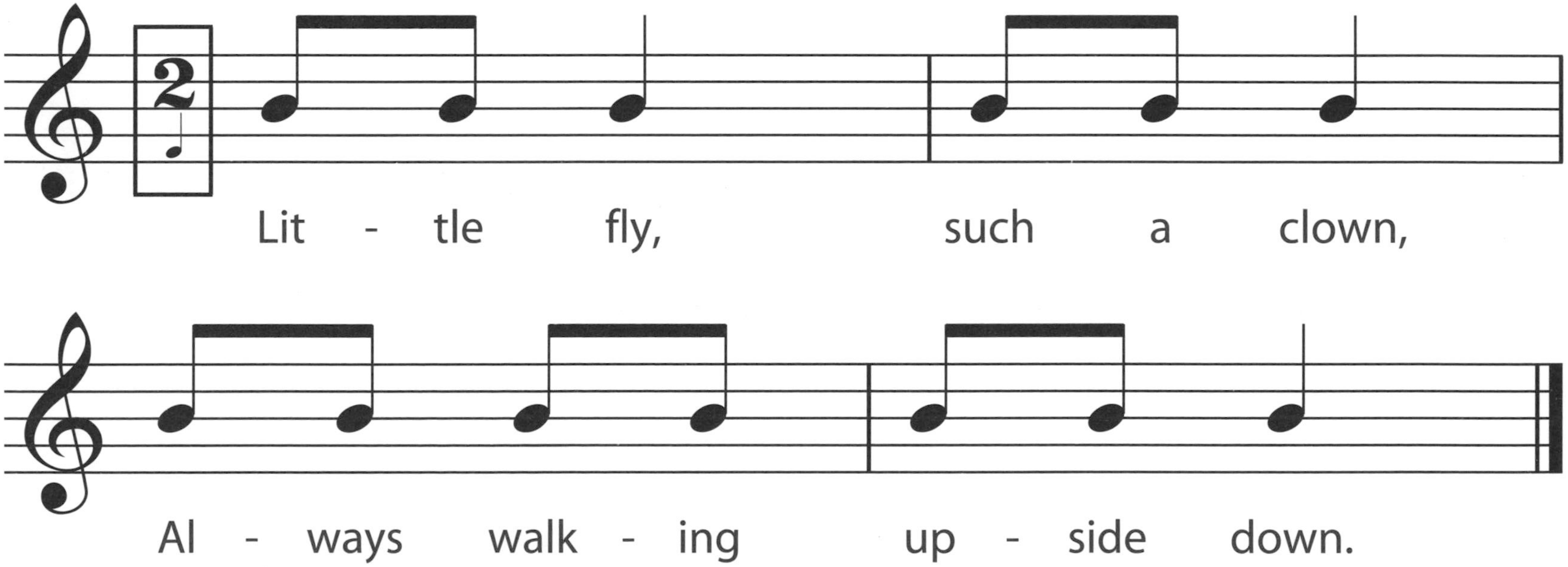

Lit - tle fly, such a clown,
Al - ways walk - ing up - side down.

No More Milk

Say and clap the words to this song.
Now play the tune using note B.

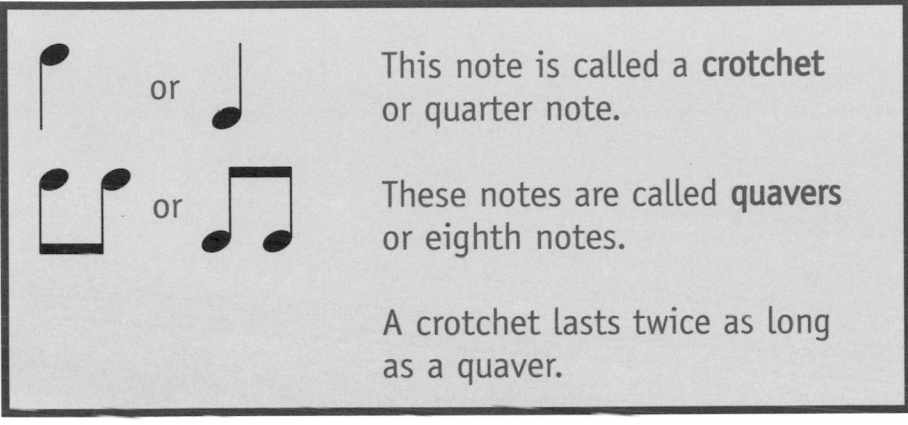

This note is called a **crotchet** or quarter note.

These notes are called **quavers** or eighth notes.

A crotchet lasts twice as long as a quaver.

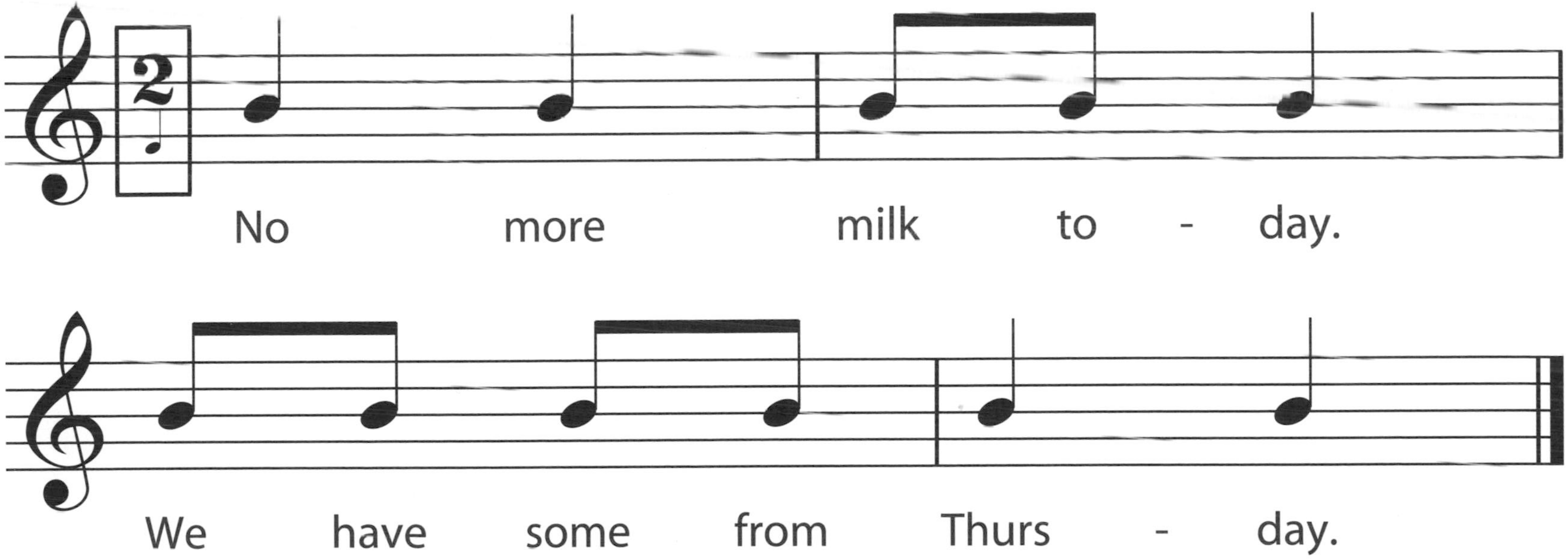

No   more   milk   to - day.

We   have   some   from   Thurs - day.

note A
B
A

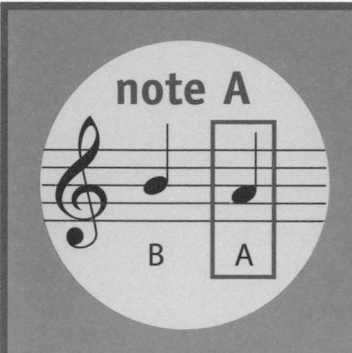

Note A

Play note B. Keep your fingers in position.
Now put your second left finger on the second hole.
Look at the diagram to help you.
This is the fingering for note A.
Play note A several times.

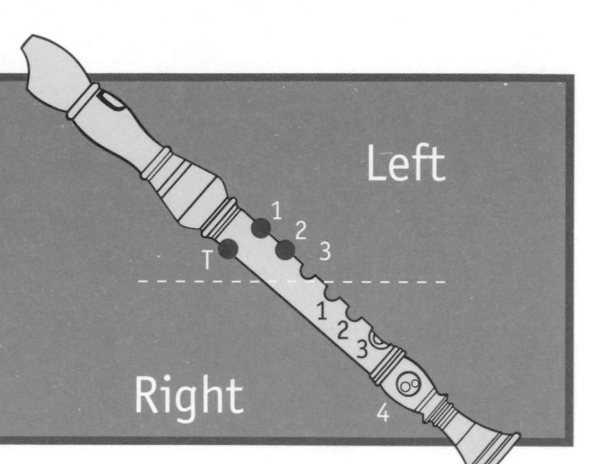

Left
1
2
T
3
1
2
3
Right
4

Traffic Jam **Words: Jan Holdstock**

Say and clap the words to this tune.
Play the tune to match the pattern of the words.

2
Lit - tle bird in the sky,
Fly - ing free, fly - ing high.

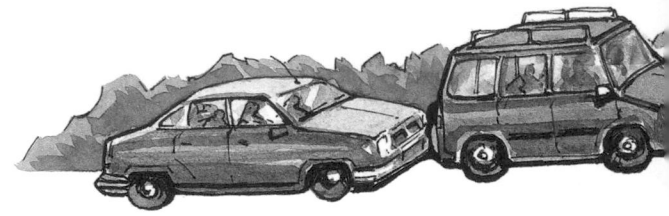

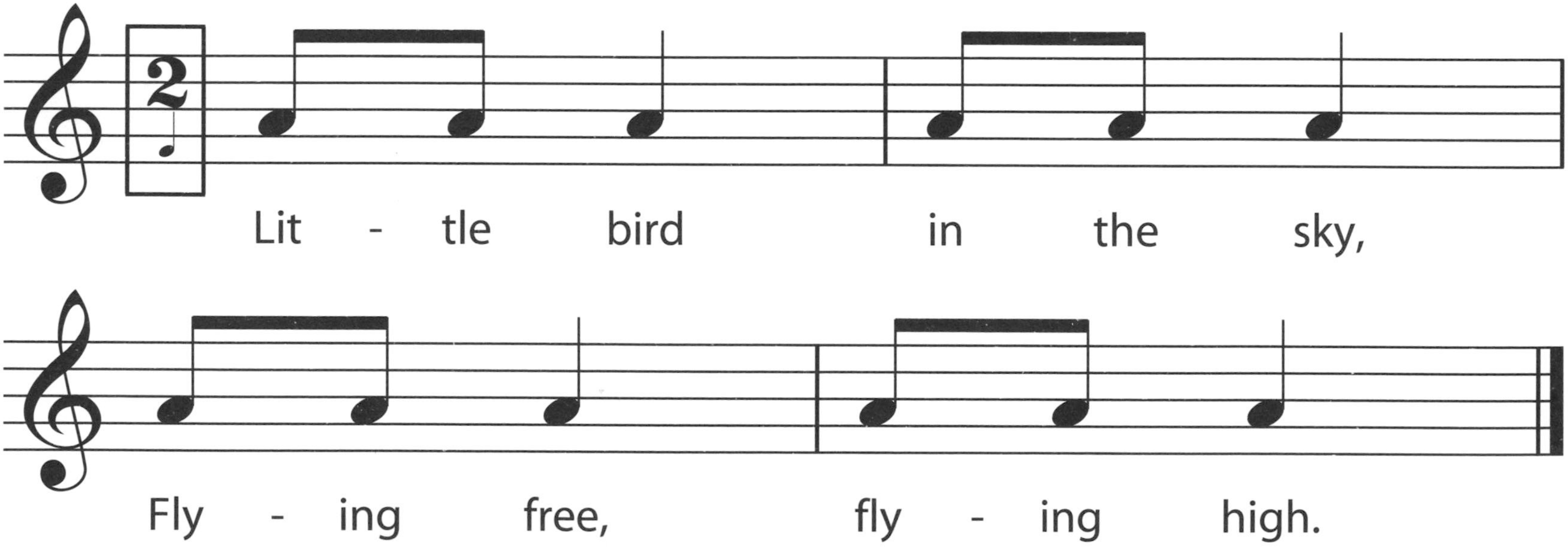

Say and clap the words before you play this tune.

Which note is used first on this page?

When you can play this tune, go back to page 8.

Play both tunes, one after the other.
This makes a long tune.

Can   you   see   just   where   I   am,

Stuck   in   a   traf - fic   jam?

Caterpillar Bye-bye

Say and clap the words, then play the tune.
Be careful not to hurry the last two notes.

Repeat sign :‖

This tells you to play all the music before the sign twice. Then you can go on.

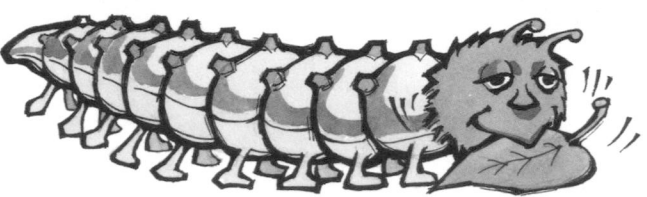

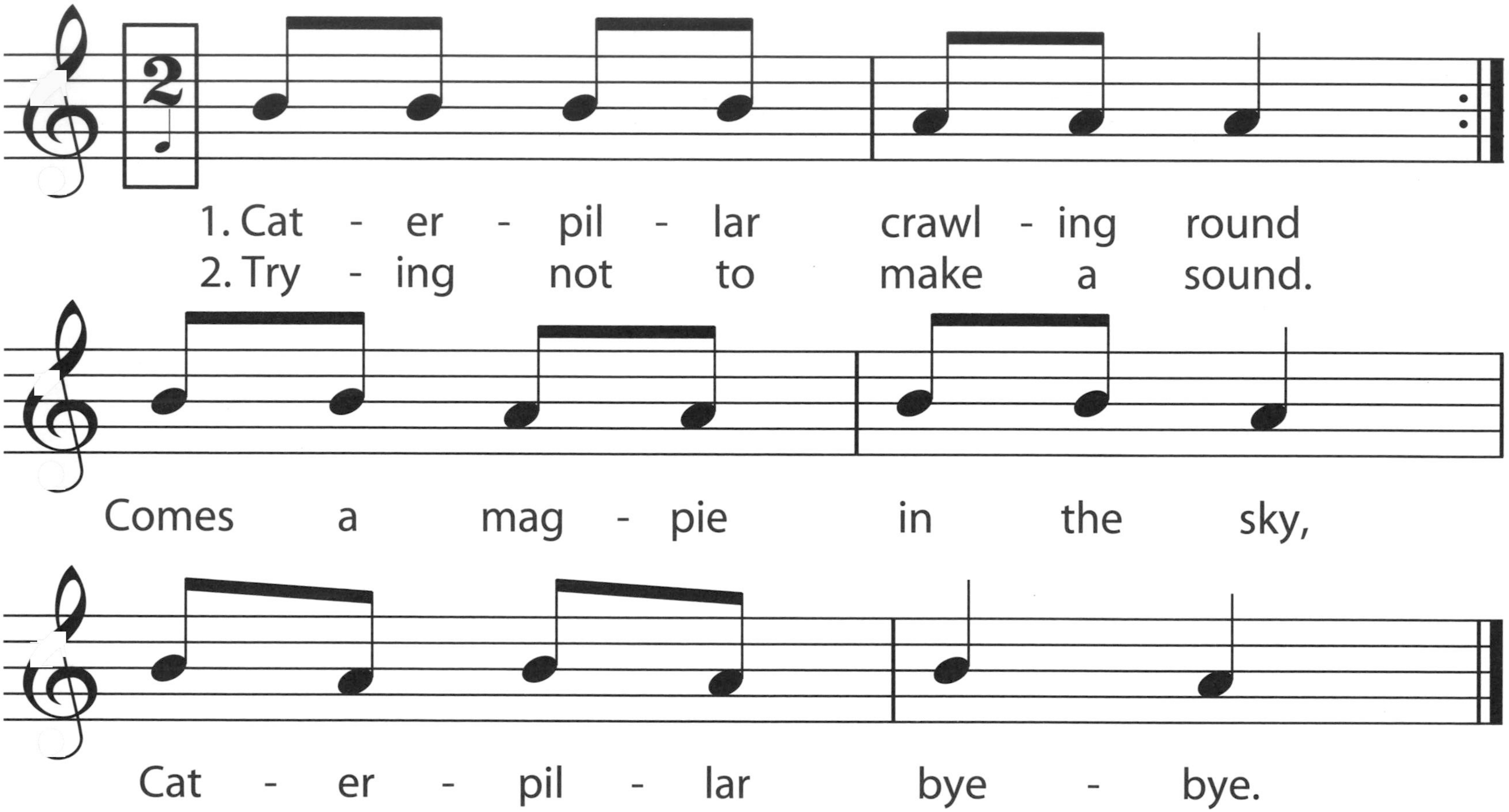

1. Cat - er - pil - lar crawl - ing round
2. Try - ing not to make a sound.
Comes a mag - pie in the sky,
Cat - er - pil - lar bye - bye.

Rhythm Game

Here are parts of some of the tunes you have learned.

Can you play them one at a time?
If you need help, turn back to the tunes.

1 (page 6)

2 (page 10)

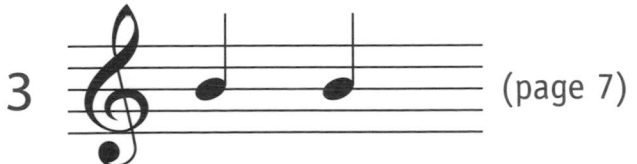

3 (page 7)

Now you can play a game with some friends.
Play either **number 1** or **number 2**.
Can your friends guess which number you played?
Let someone else play one.
Can you guess which one it was?

Play the game again using **number 2** and **number 3**.
Now make the game harder by choosing from all three tunes.

note G
A
G

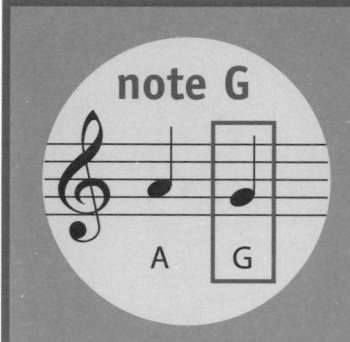

Note G

Play note A. Keep your fingers in position.
Now put your third left finger on the third hole.
Look at the diagram to help you.
This is the fingering for note G.
Play it.

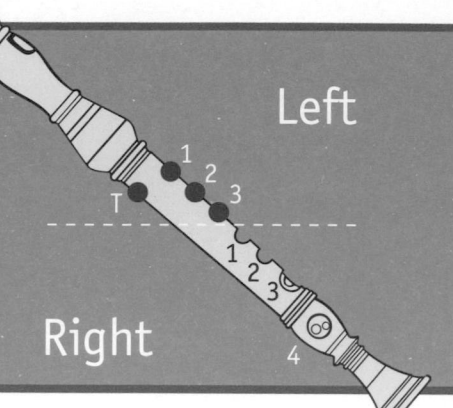

Left
T
1
2
3
1
2
3
4
Right

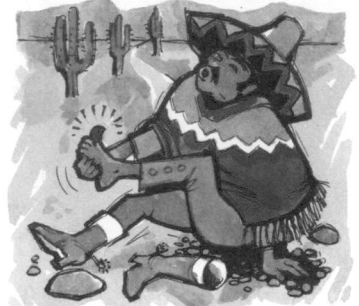

Joe, Joe

Say and clap the words of the first line. Now play the music of the first line. Do this for line 2 and line 3. Join them together and play the whole song.

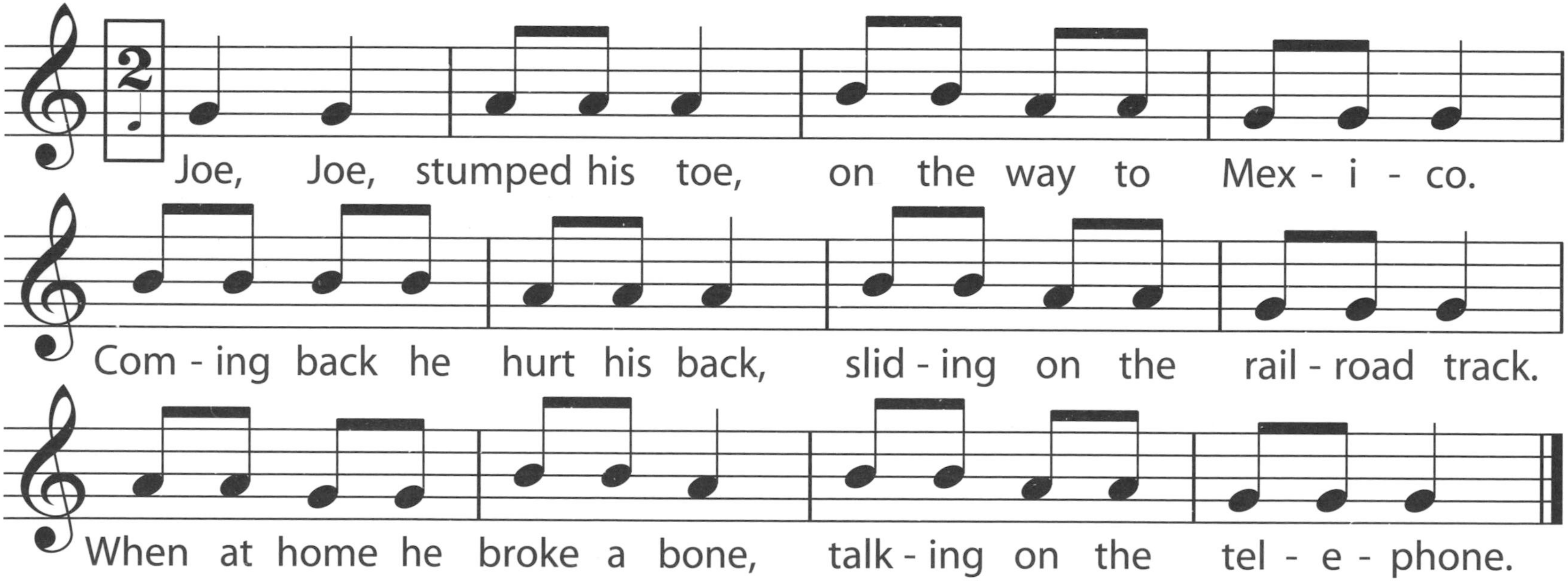

Joe, Joe, stumped his toe, on the way to Mex - i - co.
Com - ing back he hurt his back, slid - ing on the rail - road track.
When at home he broke a bone, talk - ing on the tel - e - phone.

Gypsy Dance

Count and clap each line of the tune before your play it.

Use the numbers printed above the stave. Which line has a repeat sign?

Bar lines divide tunes into groups of notes called bars.

Double bar lines show the end of a tune.

Bus Driver

Look at this sign **2** at the beginning of the tune.

It is called the **Time Signature**. It tells us to make each bar last for two crotchet (quarter note) beats.

This tune uses a new note which looks like this: ♩

It is called a **minim** or half note.
A minim lasts as long as two crotchets (quarter notes).

Say and clap the words, then play the tune.
To clap a minim say "clap-press" (and do it!)
This takes the time of two beats.

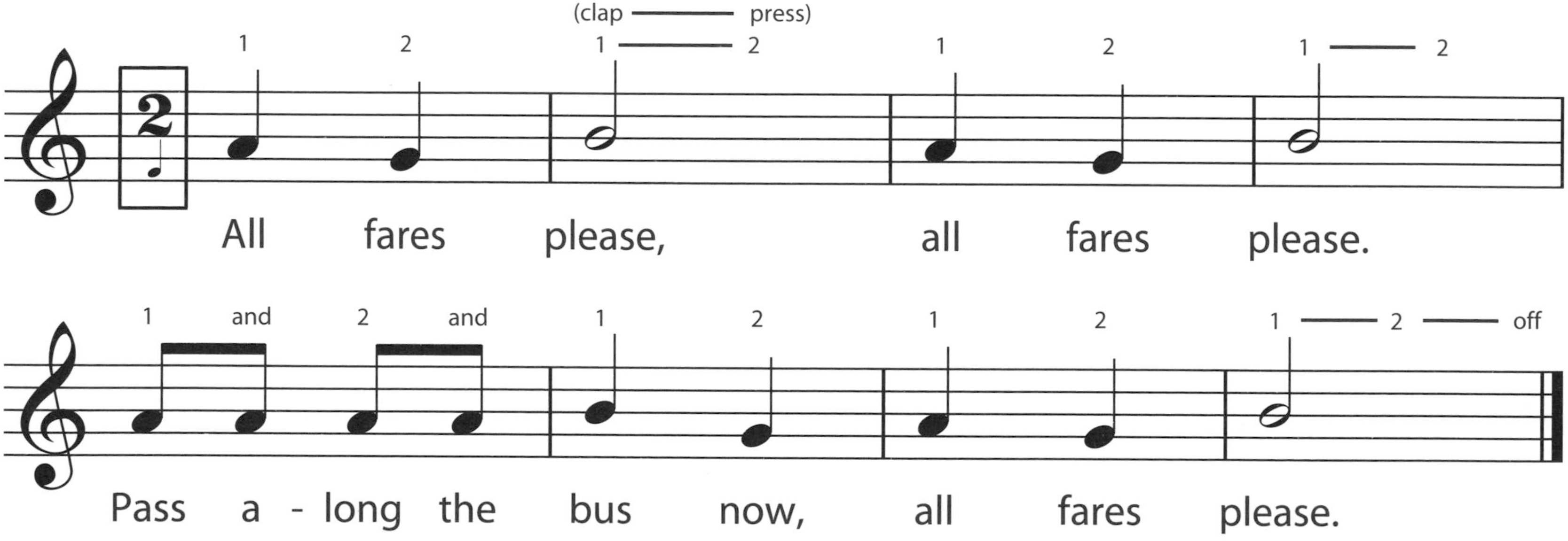

All fares please, all fares please.

Pass a - long the bus now, all fares please.

Traffic Lights

Tongue each note (say "tu") when you play this tune.

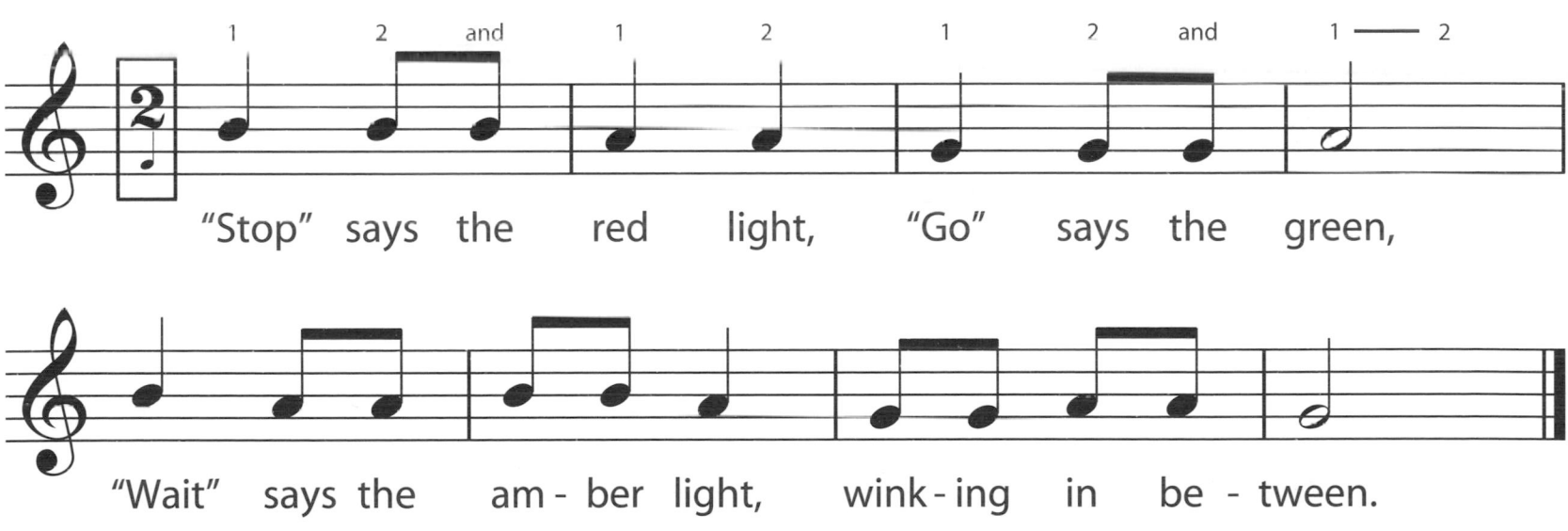

"Stop" says the red light, "Go" says the green,

"Wait" says the am - ber light, wink - ing in be - tween.

Hot Cross Buns

This tune has four crotchet beats in each bar.
What tells us this? The Time Signature.
Count and clap before you play the tune.

Sometimes quavers (eighth notes) are joined together in twos:

Sometimes they are joined together in fours:

They are both played exactly the same.

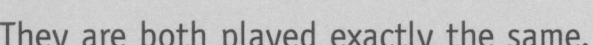

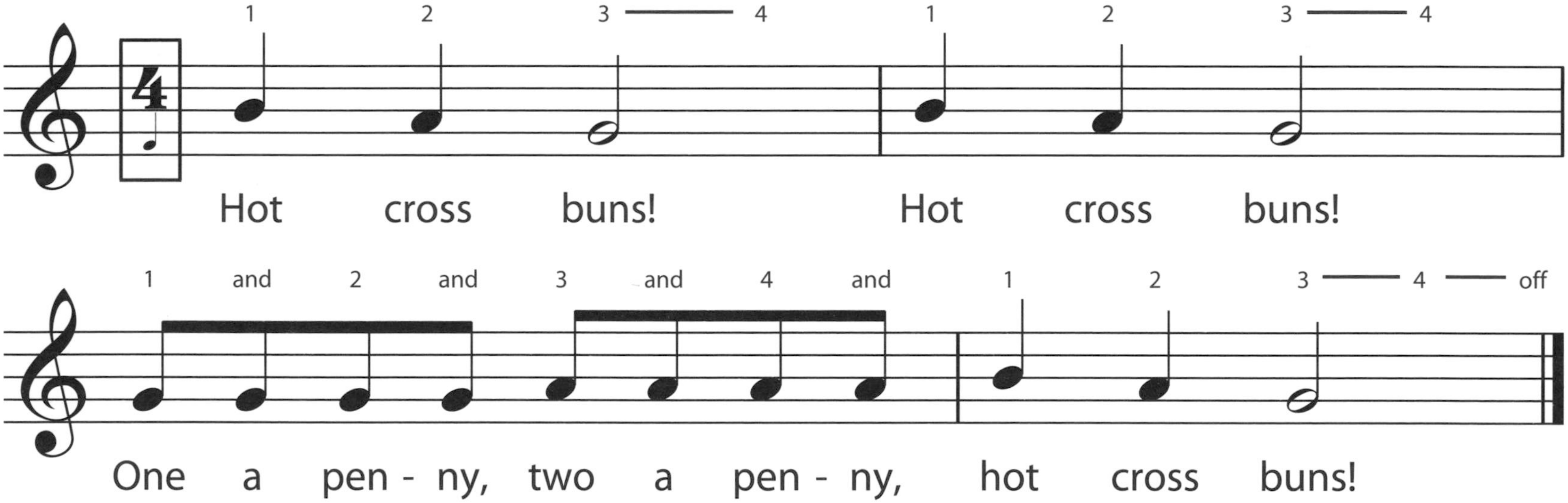

| | 1 | 2 | 3 — 4 | 1 | 2 | 3 — 4 |

Hot   cross   buns!   Hot   cross   buns!

| 1 | and | 2 | and | 3 | and | 4 | and | 1 | 2 | 3 — 4 — off |

One   a   pen - ny,   two   a   pen - ny,   hot   cross   buns!

For extra tunes using the notes and rhythms met so far, see *Recorder from the Beginning* **Tune Book 1**.

Who's That Yonder?

This tune has a new sign in it:

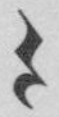

It means make no sound for one beat.
It is called a **crotchet rest** (quarter note rest).

Count, clap and play this exercise.
Then play the tune.

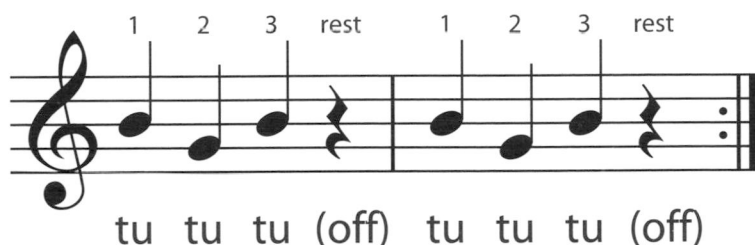

1 2 3 rest 1 2 3 rest
tu tu tu (off) tu tu tu (off)

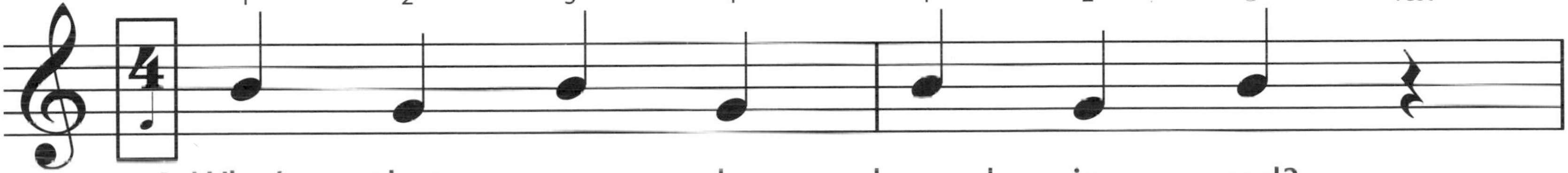

1 2 3 4 1 2 3 rest
1. Who's that yon der dressed in red?
2. Who's that yon - der dressed in white?

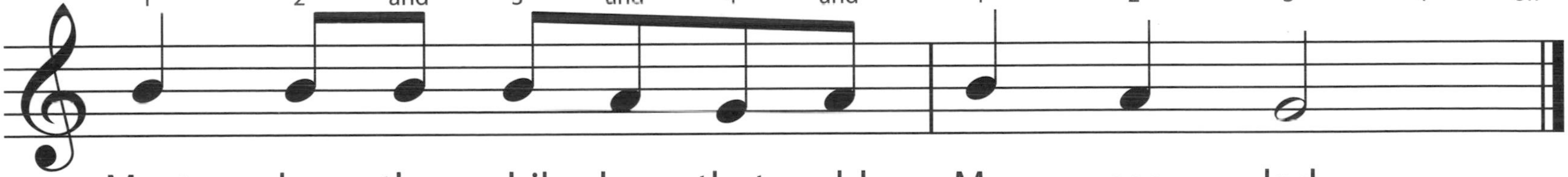

1 2 and 3 and 4 and 1 2 3 —— 4 —— off
Must be the chil - dren that old Mo - ses led.
Must be the chil - dren of the Is - rael - ite.

Kites

Here is a tune with three beats in each bar.

Each line ends with a dotted note 𝅗𝅥. worth three beats.

Count and play the tune.

Now read the explanation at the bottom of this page.

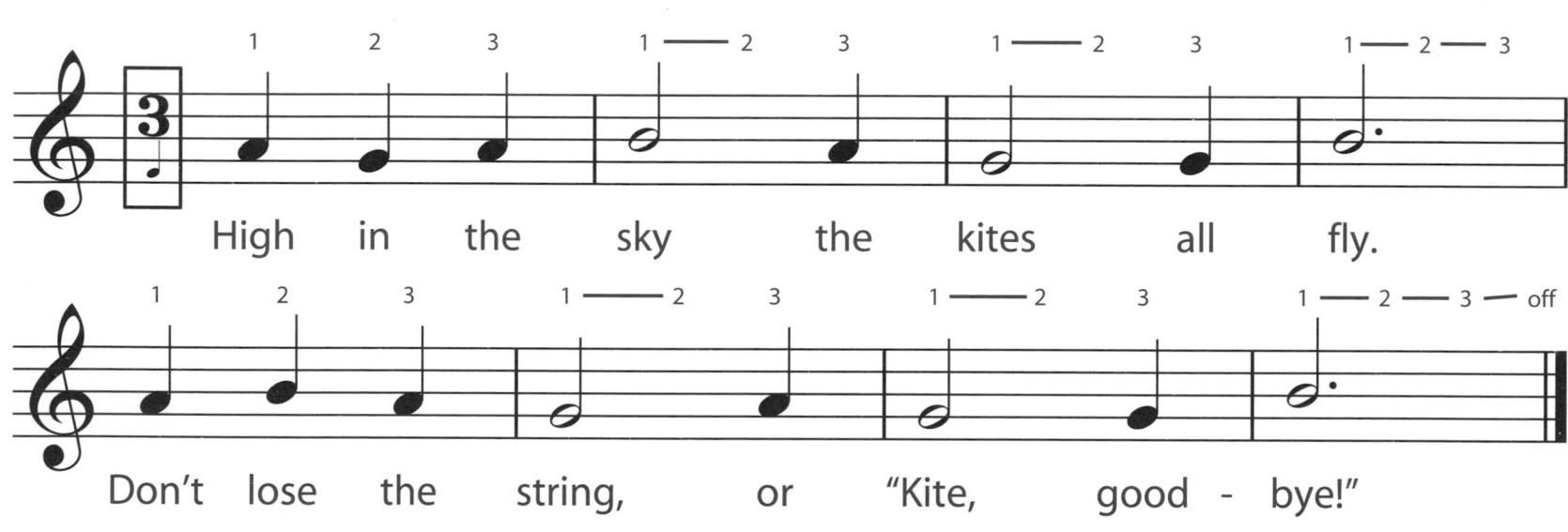

A dot after a note tells us to add half the value of the note. 𝅗𝅥. = 𝅗𝅥 + ♩

So 𝅗𝅥. lasts for 3 beats. To clap 𝅗𝅥. go "clap-press-press".   3 = 2 + 1

Gliding

This sign ✓ shows you where to take a breath.

Only take breaths at breathing places marked ✓

When you can play this tune, go back to page 18. Join both tunes together to make one long tune.

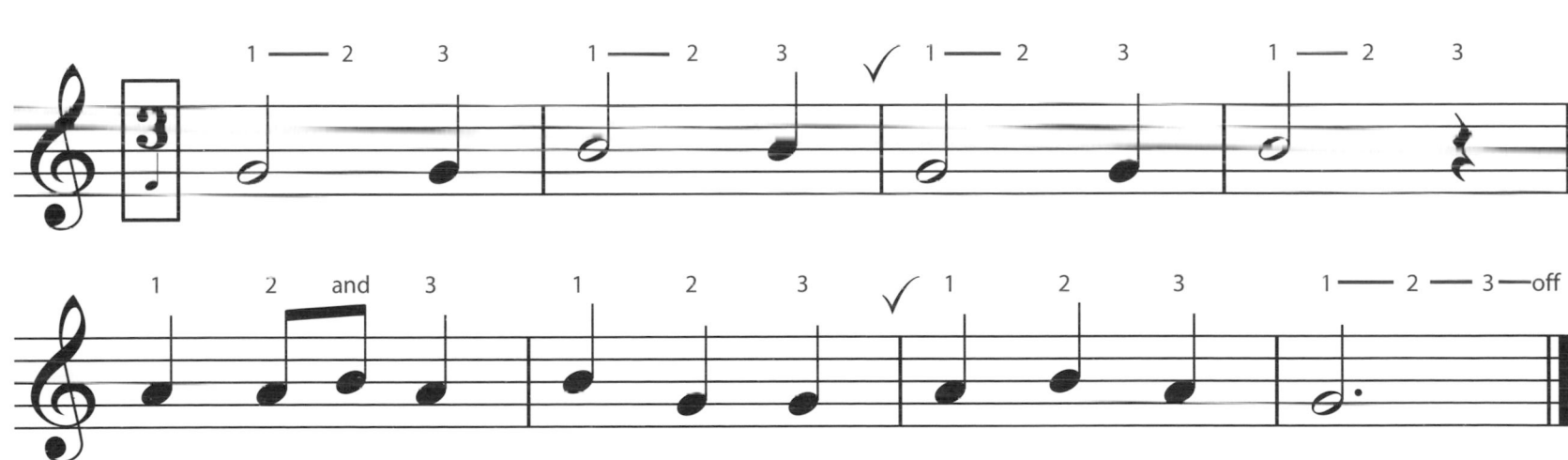

Note E

Play note G. Keep your fingers in position.
Now put the first and second fingers of
your right hand on the next two holes.
Look at the diagram to help you.
This is the fingering for note E.
Play it.

note E

G   E

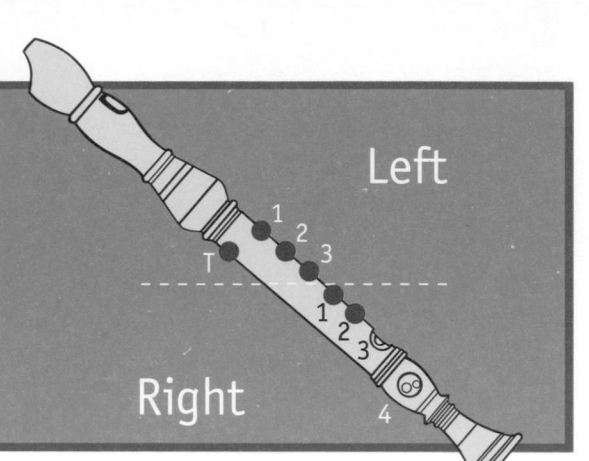

Left

Right

Elephants

Now play the last two bars of the tune.
Then play all the tune

Hump,   wump,   dump,   chump

El – eph – ants   walk   with   an   aw – ful   bump.

When you can play this tune well, divide into two groups. One group plays "awful bump" (the last two bars) again and again. This is called an **ostinato** accompaniment.
The other group plays the tune. Someone must count, "1–2–3" so that both groups begin together.
Repeat the tune and the groups can change parts.

Indian Warrior

Say and clap the words, then play the tune.

I'm   an   In - dian   war - ri - or,   war - ri - or,

Big   Chief   In - dian   war - ri - or,   war - ri - or

Hi   ho!   Hi   ho!

Hi   Hi,   Hi   ho!

A New Rhythm

Count and clap this short tune.
Then play it.

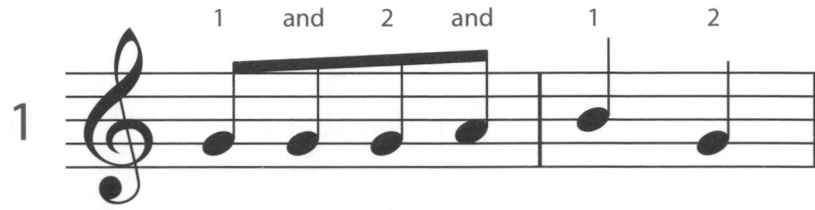

1

Here is the tune again, with one difference. This time it uses the **tie** sign ‿
When two notes are tied together, do not play the second note.
Hold the first note for the value of both notes added together.
It makes a longer sound.

2

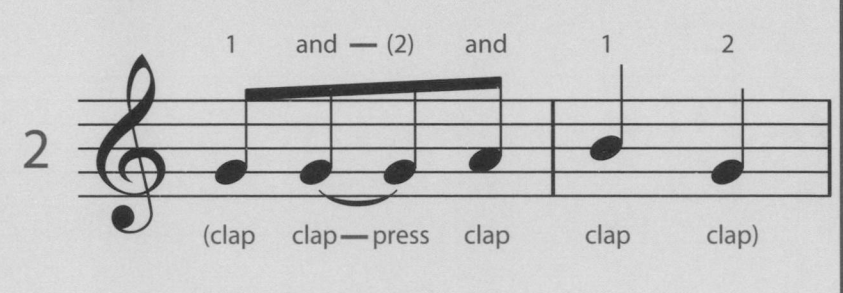

Count and clap **tune 2**, then play it. Remember to hold the tied note.

Tune 3 is another way of writing **tune 2**.
Tune 3 uses a quarter note (crotchet) in place of two eighth notes (quavers).
We could do this because the eighth notes were tied together.

3

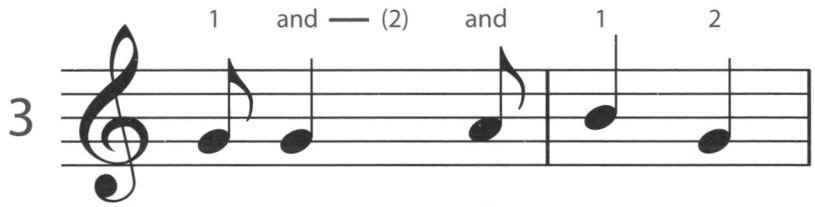

Play **tune 3**.
Make it sound exactly the same as **tune 2**.

Skateboard Ride begins with **tune 3**.
Can you find **tune 3** anywhere else in *Skateboard Ride*?

Play the whole 'Ride'.

22

Skateboard Ride

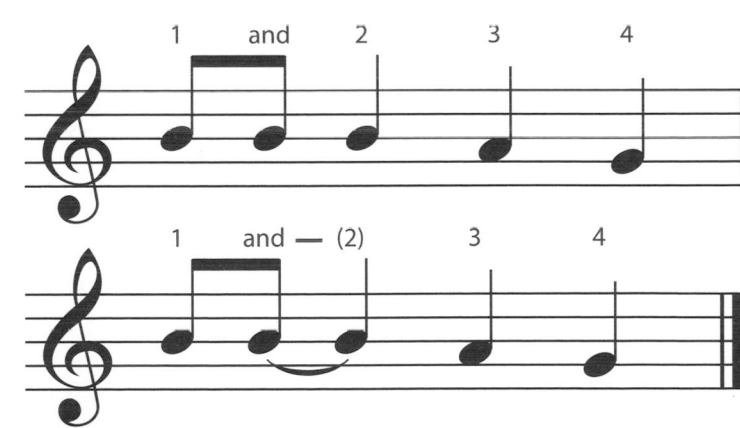

The tune on the next page also uses tied notes.
Here they are to practise before you play the tune.
Count and clap, then play this line.

Count and clap, then play.
Remember to hold the tied note.

Chicka Hanka — a 'blues' tune

This tune uses two new signs.
Both are worth four beats.

○ is called a **semibreve** or whole note. It keeps sounding for four beats.

▬ is called a **semibreve rest** or whole note rest. It means silence, or rest, for four beats.

Practise the first line before you play the whole tune.

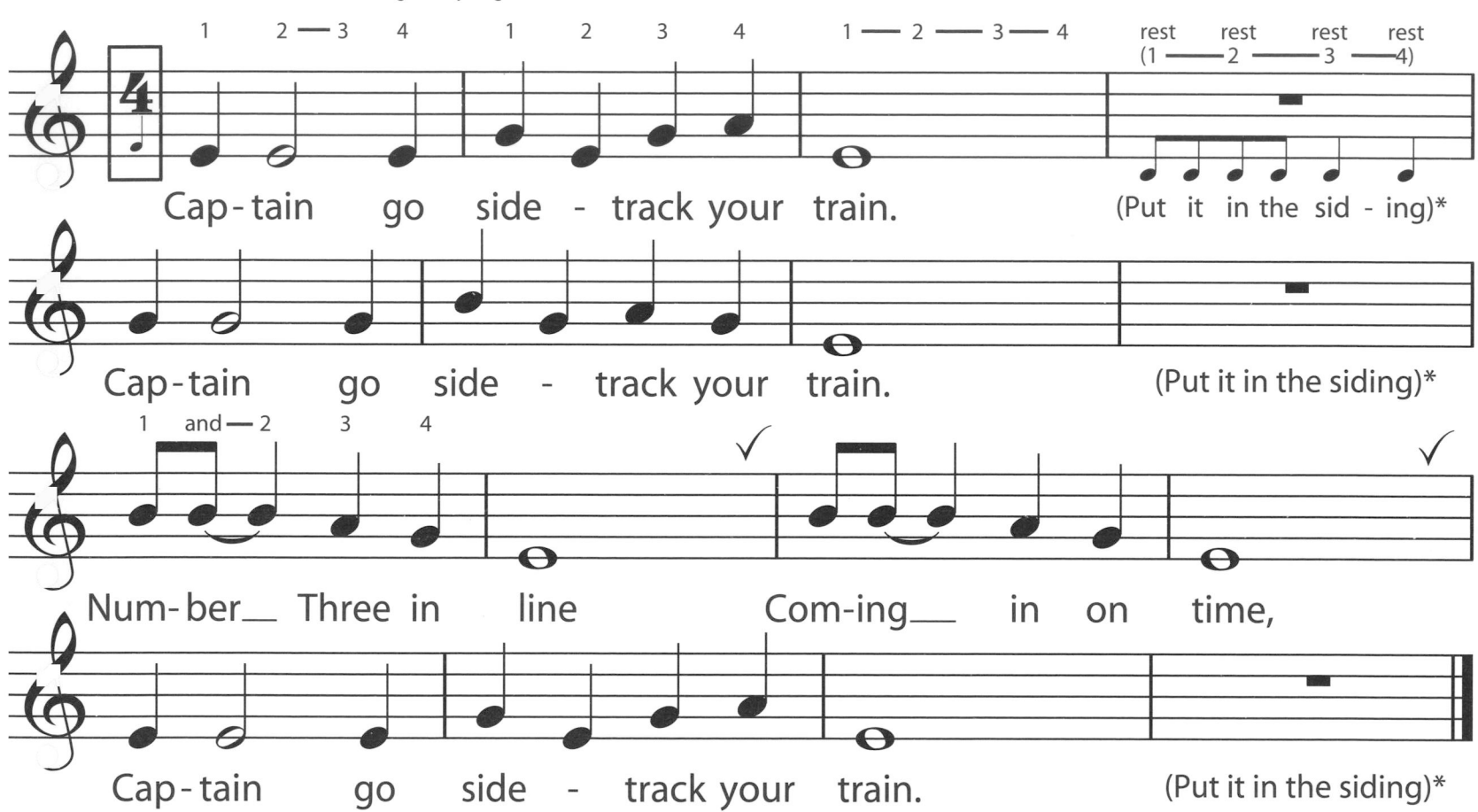

Cap-tain   go   side - track your train.   (Put it in the sid - ing)*

Cap-tain   go   side - track your train.   (Put it in the siding)*

Num-ber__ Three in   line   Com-ing__ in on   time,

Cap-tain   go   side - track your train.   (Put it in the siding)*

*Say these words, but do not play them. They will help you to keep time.

Fandango — a Spanish dance

Can you find any bars that are the same as each other?
Which line is the same as line 2?
Now play the tune.

When you can play the tune well, use this rhythm **ostinato**
(repeating pattern) to make an accompaniment.
Count and clap it. Try saying the words to help you. Then
divide into two groups.
Group 1 plays the rhythm ostinato on tambourine or claves.
Group 2 plays the tune on their recorders. Then change round.

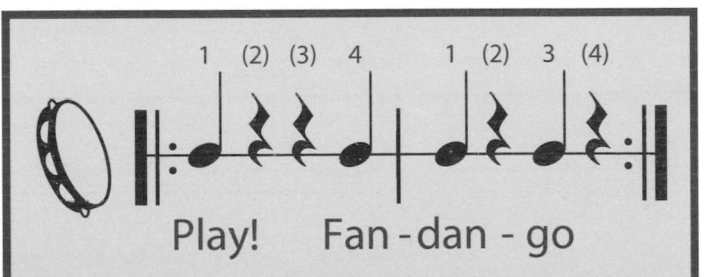

1 (2) (3) 4   1 (2) 3 (4)

Play!   Fan - dan - go

25

Note D

Play note E. Keep our fingers in position.
Now put the third finger of your right hand
on the next hole hole.
Use the diagram to help you.
This is the fingering for note D. Play it.

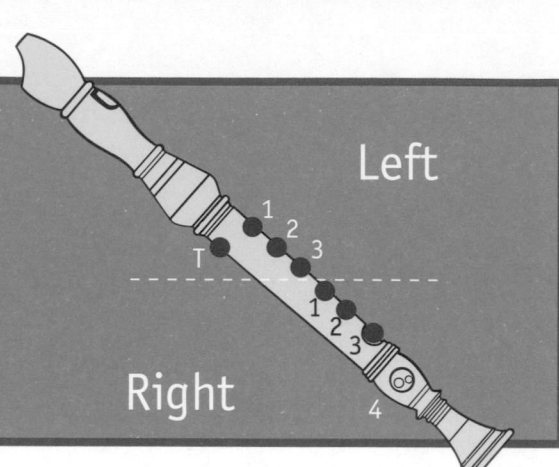

Left

Right

Chatter With The Angels

Tied Notes

Remember (page 22) that when two
notes are tied we do play the
second note.
We add its value to the first note.
Play both these tunes and listen to
the difference.

Chat-ter with the an-gels soon in the morn-ing, Chat-ter with the an-gels { in that land.
                                                                                { join that band.

I   hope___ to   join that band and chat-ter with the an-gels   all day long.

Cameron's Spaceship

Can you play this tune without stopping at all? When you can, divide into two groups and play the tune as a **round**. One group starts first. When they have finished playing all the first line, the other group starts to play from the beginning. Each group stops when they have played the whole tune twice.

Class activity
A group of singers can be Group 1, with Recorders as Group 2.

Take me in your space-ship to the moon, zoom - ing fast we'll get there soon.

A Bring me home a-gain if it's too far, I'll___ go back in my Dad's car!

The next tune uses some **slurred** notes.
The slur sign is a curved line, rather like a tie sign.
But a **slur** joins different notes.
To play two notes which are slurred together, tongue the first note but not the second.
Keep blowing, but change the fingering to make the second note.
The slur joins different notes together smoothly.
Be careful not to mix up slurred notes and tied notes.
Practise these slurs which use parts of the tune.

tongue slur tu____ tu____ tu tu____ tu

Karen's Waltz

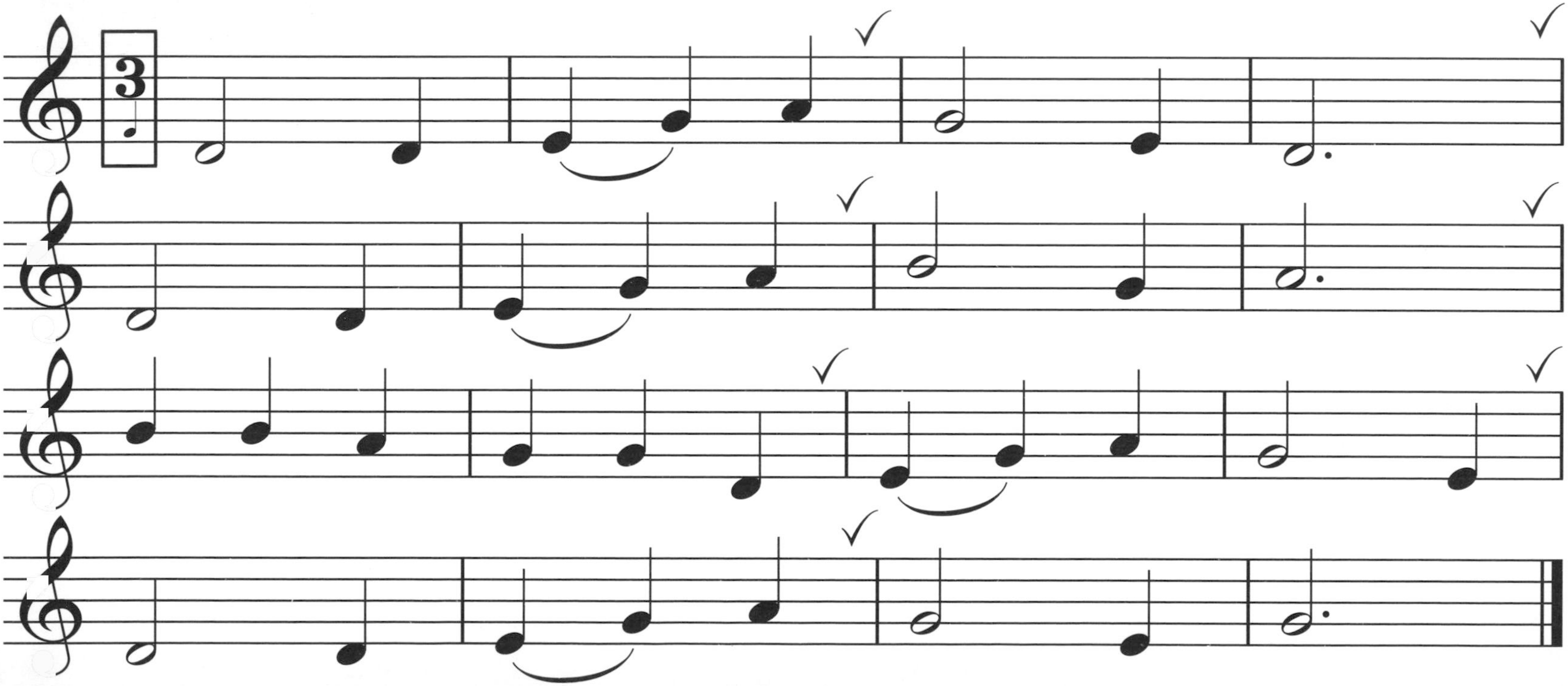

Now play *Adele's Waltz*.
Be careful with the slurs.
When you can play all the tune without any mistakes, you may read the special upside-down message!

Karen and Adele are twin sisters. Adele's Waltz is a special tune that fits with Karen's Waltz.
Divide into two groups and play both tunes at the same time.
Someone must count 1-2-3 so that both groups start exactly together.
When one tune fits with another tune, we call the music a **duet**.

Adele's Waltz

Old MacDonald

Old Mac-Don-ald had a farm, E I E I Oh! And

on that farm he had some chicks E I E I Oh! With a

Repeat these 4 bars as necessary as you add more animals.

cluck, cluck here and a cluck, cluck there, Here a cluck, there a cluck, ev-'ry-where a cluck, cluck.

Old Mac-Don-ald had a farm, E I E I Oh!

2 pigs (oink, oink)
3 sheep (baa, baa)
4 cows (moo, moo)
5 turkeys (gobble, gobble)

Rhythm Game

Here are some bars from the tune *Old MacDonald*.

Practise each bar, and then choose one to play to your friends.

Can your friends guess which bar you played?

The person who guessed right has the next turn.

1

2

3

Pitch Game

Here are some more bars from *Old MacDonald*.

(Pitch means how high or low a note is.)
Listen very carefully while someone plays tune **1** or **2**. Which was it?
How could you tell which bar was played? (Don't watch fingers!)
Later try with **3** and **4**. Then choose from all the tunes.

Which is it?
1 or **2**?

Which is it?
3 or **4**?

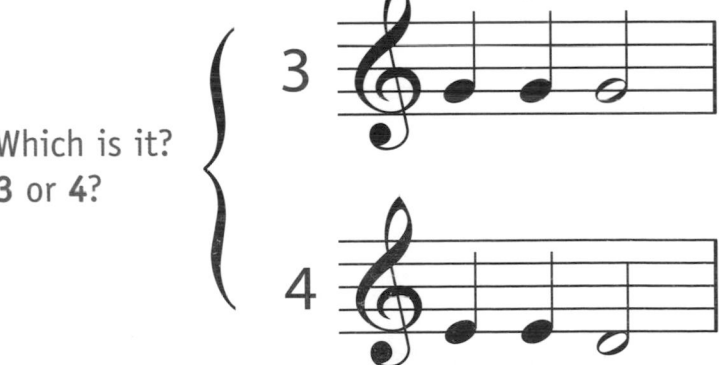

Staccato Notes

Sometimes we meet notes with a dot above or below them.
This tells us to play the notes **staccato**, or cut off short.
To do this, say "tut" instead of "tu" when tonguing.

Play these.

tut tut tut tut   tut tut tut (off)

Now see if you can play staccato–smoothly–staccato–smoothly.
Be careful to give full value to notes which are not staccato.

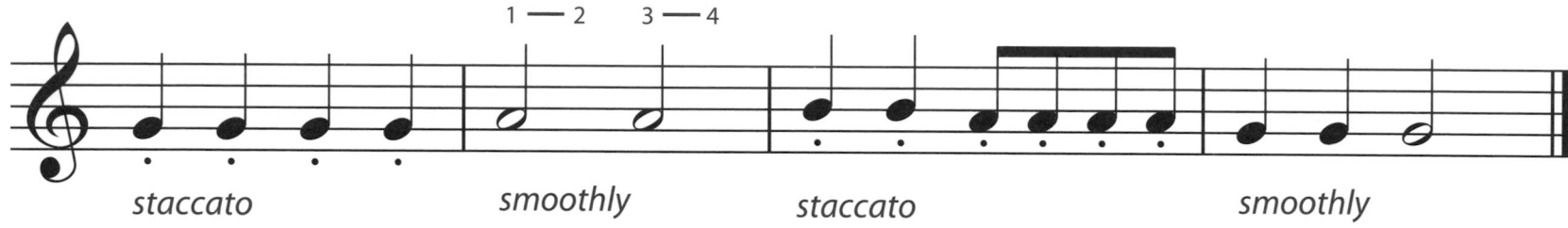

staccato   *smoothly*   *staccato*   *smoothly*

The tune on the next page uses staccato notes and slurs.
Here they are to practise.

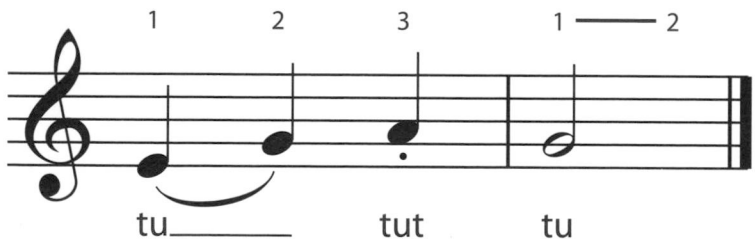

tu_____ tut tu

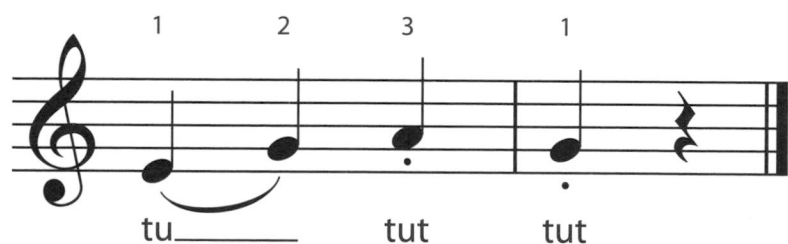

tu_____ tut tut

Now find them in the tune and play them again.

For other tunes using slurred and staccato notes, see
Recorder From The Beginning **Tune Book 1.**

Dear Liza

Most of this tune is similar to the first line.
Notice that the tune begins on count 3.
Say 1–2 and begin to play on 3.

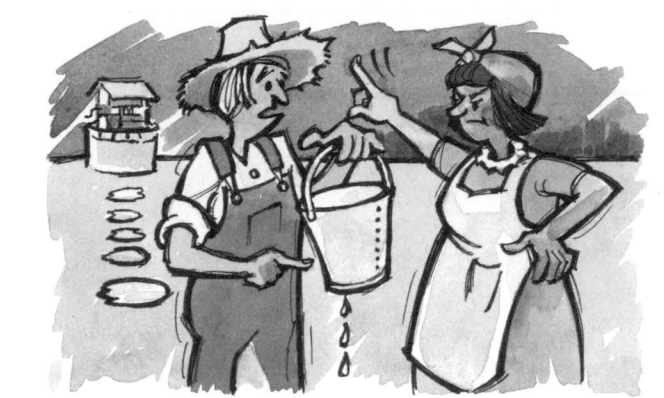

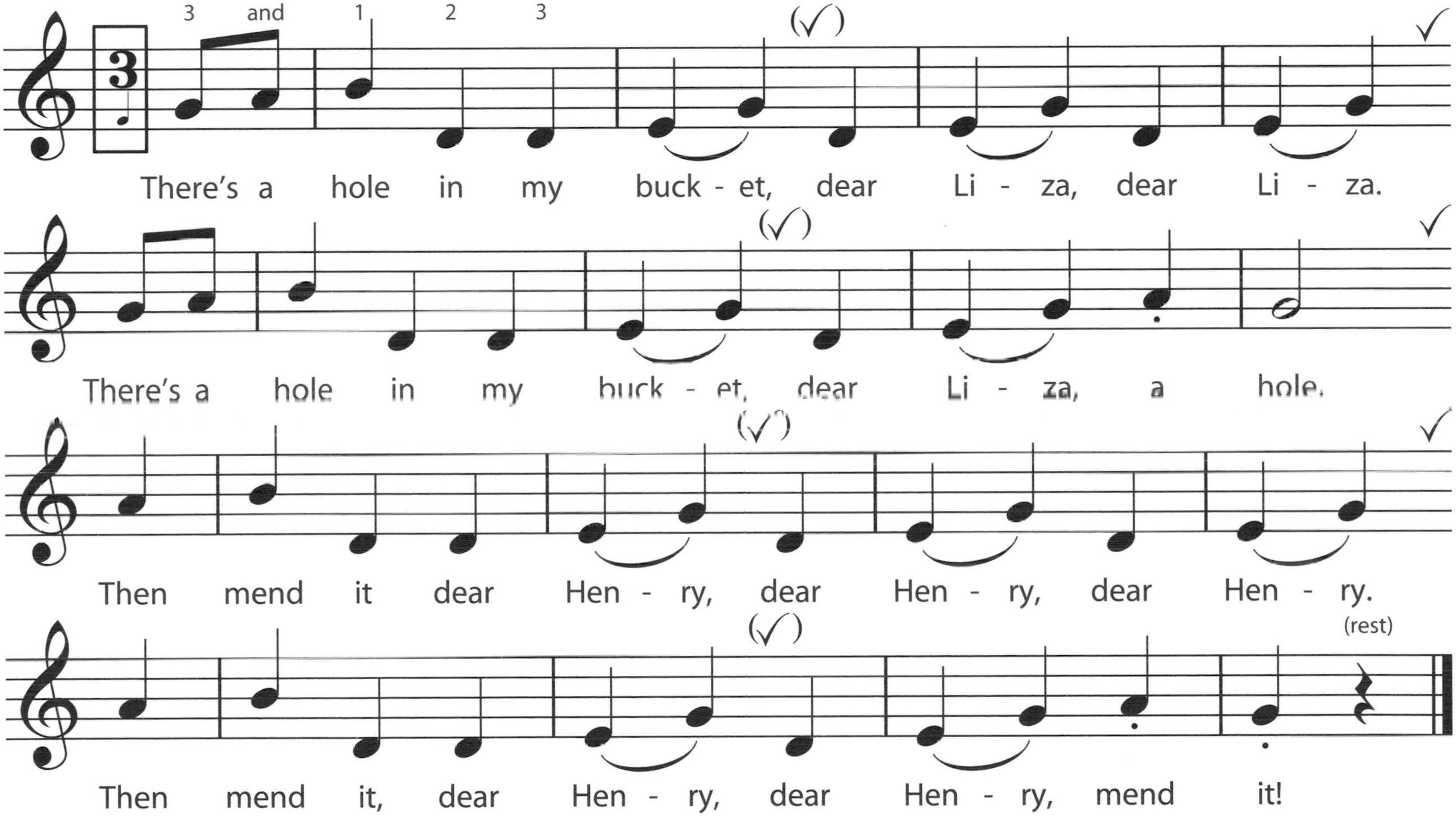

3 and 1 2 3
(✓) ✓
There's a hole in my buck - et, dear Li - za, dear Li - za.
There's a hole in my buck - et, dear Li - za, a hole.
Then mend it dear Hen - ry, dear Hen - ry, dear Hen - ry.
(rest)
Then mend it, dear Hen - ry, dear Hen - ry, mend it!

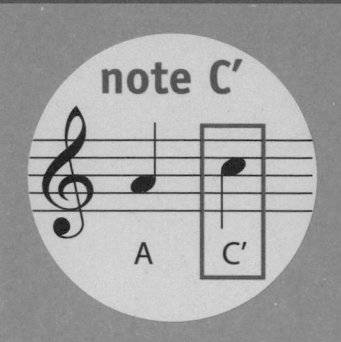

note C′
A
C′

Note C′ (upper C)

Play note A. Then take off your left first finger. Keep your second finger and thumb covering the holes.
Look at the diagram to help you.
This is note C′ (upper C). Play it.

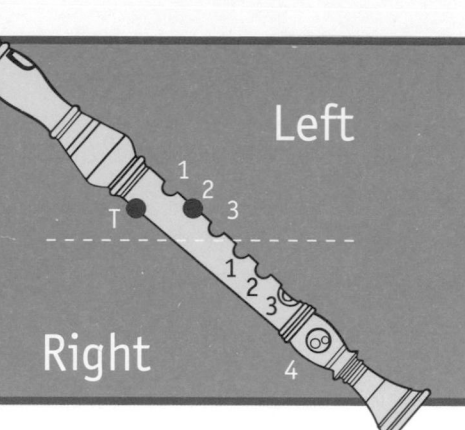

Left
1
2
T
3
1
2
3
Right
4

Tadpoles **Words: Rose Fyleman**

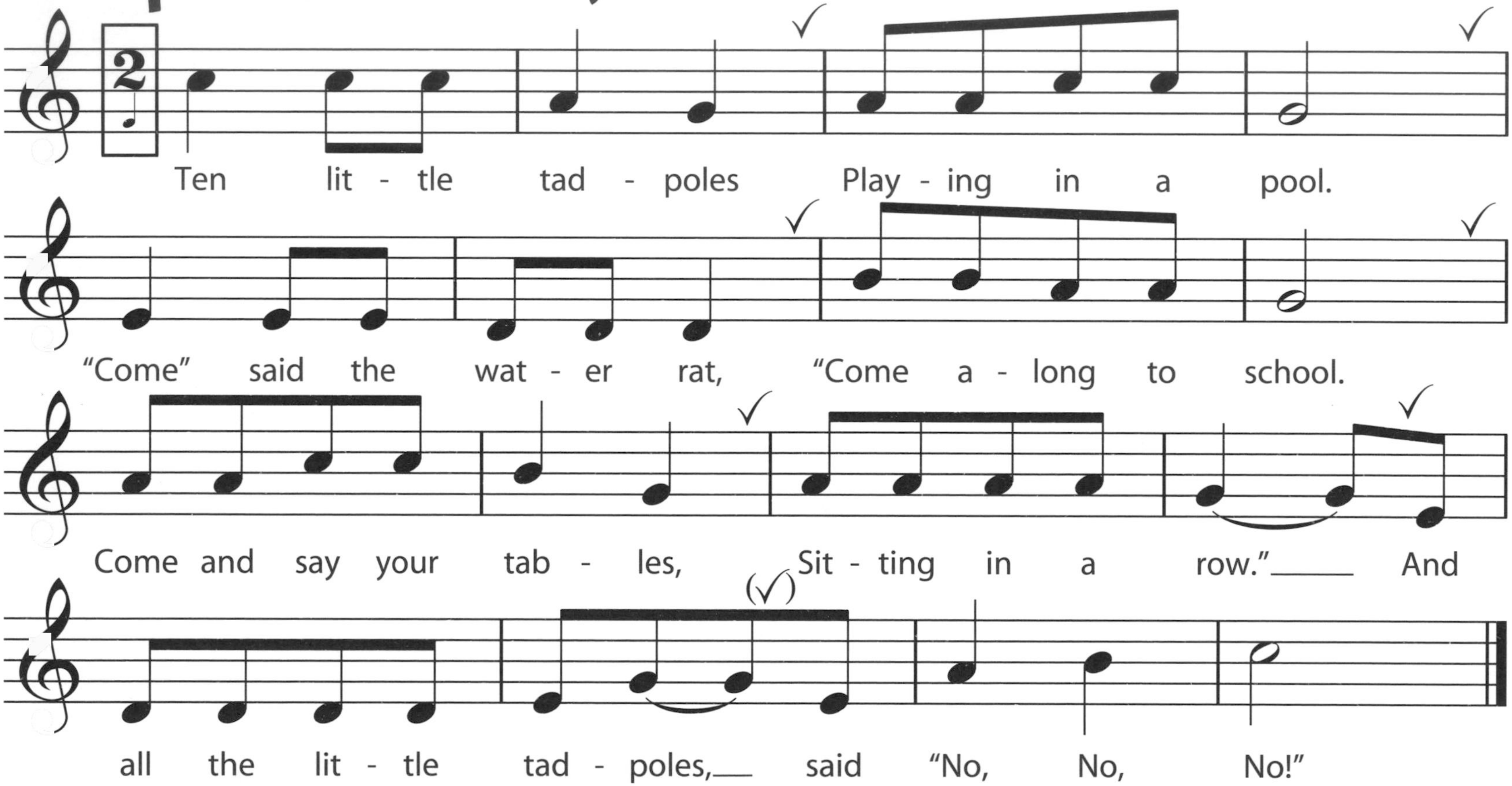

2
Ten lit - tle tad - poles Play - ing in a pool.
"Come" said the wat - er rat, "Come a - long to school.
Come and say your tab - les, Sit - ting in a row." And
all the lit - tle tad - poles, said "No, No, No!"

Scarecrow

When you can play the tune twice without stopping, play it as a **round**. Divide into two groups. Group 1 starts and when they have played all the first line, Group 2 joins in from the beginning. Each group stops when they have played the whole tune twice.

Class activity
A group of singers can be Group 1, with Recorders as Group 2.

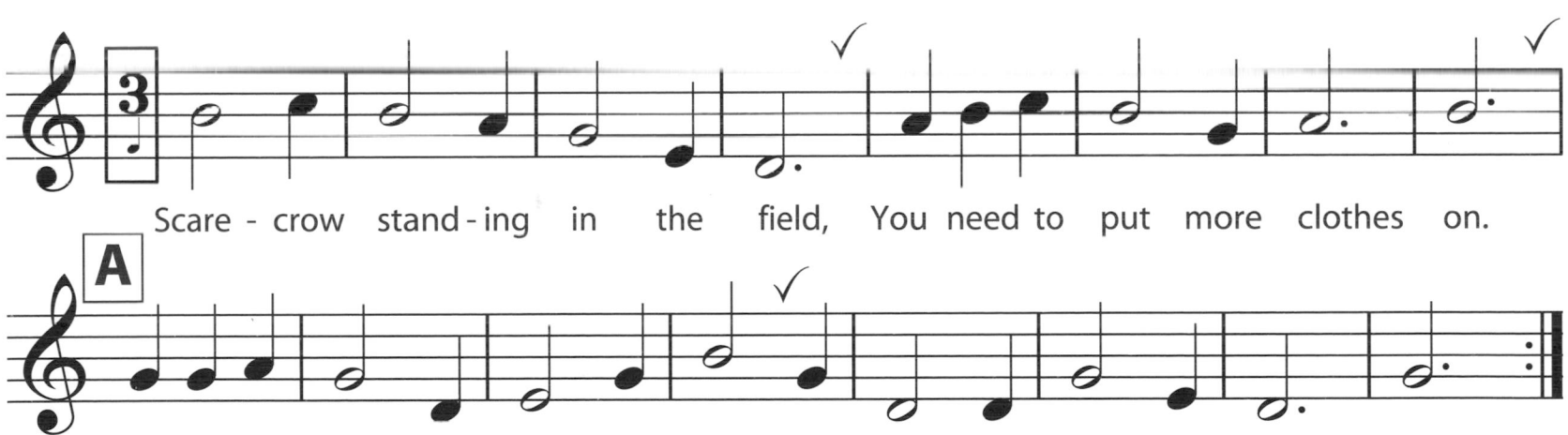

Scare - crow stand - ing in the field, You need to put more clothes on.

A When the wind blows the crows all know, That you can't keep your hat on!

Who Built The Ark?

Fine (pronounced 'fee-nay') means the end of the tune. For **D.C.** see page 43.

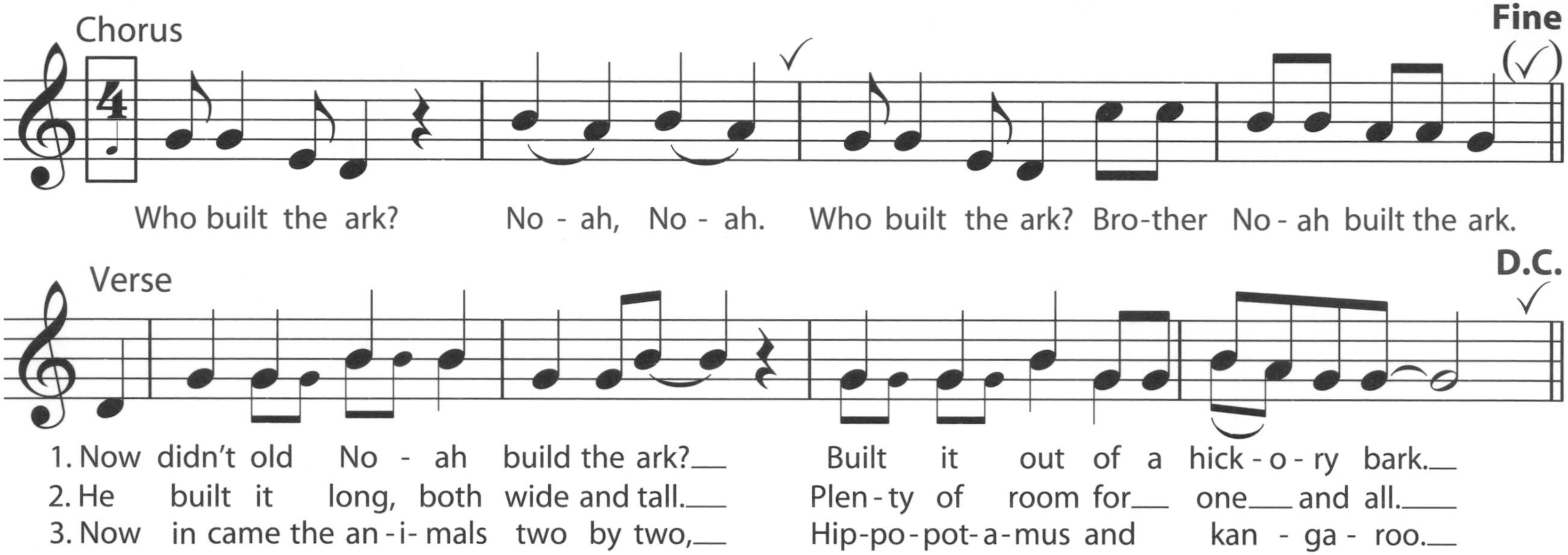

Chorus   **Fine**

Who built the ark?   No - ah, No - ah.   Who built the ark? Bro-ther No - ah built the ark.

Verse   **D.C.**

1. Now didn't old No - ah build the ark?___   Built it out of a hick - o - ry bark.___
2. He built it long, both wide and tall.___   Plen - ty of room for___ one___ and all.___
3. Now in came the an - i - mals two by two,___   Hip-po-pot-a-mus and kan - ga - roo.___

Mocking Bird

Hush lit-tle ba - by don't say a word, Mam - my's going to buy you a mock - ing bird.

If that mock -ing bird won't sing, Mam - my's going to buy you a dia - mond ring.

Harrison's Rag

The first bar of this tune uses the same rhythm as *Skateboard Ride* on page 23.

What do you notice about the music of line 2 and line 4 of this tune? Are any other parts the same?

More About Rhythm

Tango Zanjitas on page 39 uses a new way of writing the rhythm
You played this rhythm in *Tadpoles* on page 34.

Let us practise before playing the tune.
Tangos always include this rhythm.

Clap and count, then play.

1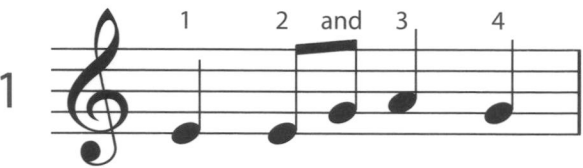

Remember when two notes are **tied** you do not play the
second note. Add its value to the first note.

2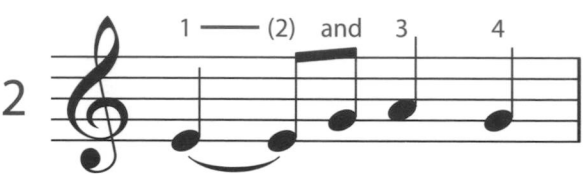

> Here is another way to write the same rhythm.
> The dot after the note makes the note half as
> long again.
> So 2 and 3 should sound exactly the same.
>
> 3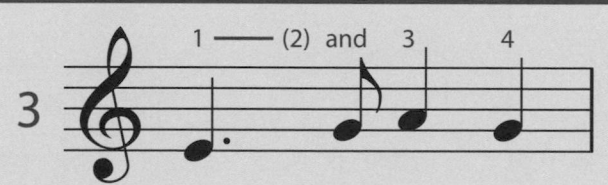

Now you have played the rhythm of the first bar of the Tango.
Can you find six more bars in the tune that use the same rhythm,
but with different notes?
Play them and then play the tune.

Tango Zanjitas

Mobile Phone

When you can play this tune, try it as a **round** using two groups. Both groups can be recorders, or one group can be singers. Group 2 starts from the beginning when Group 1 reaches the 2nd line. Each group performs the round twice through.

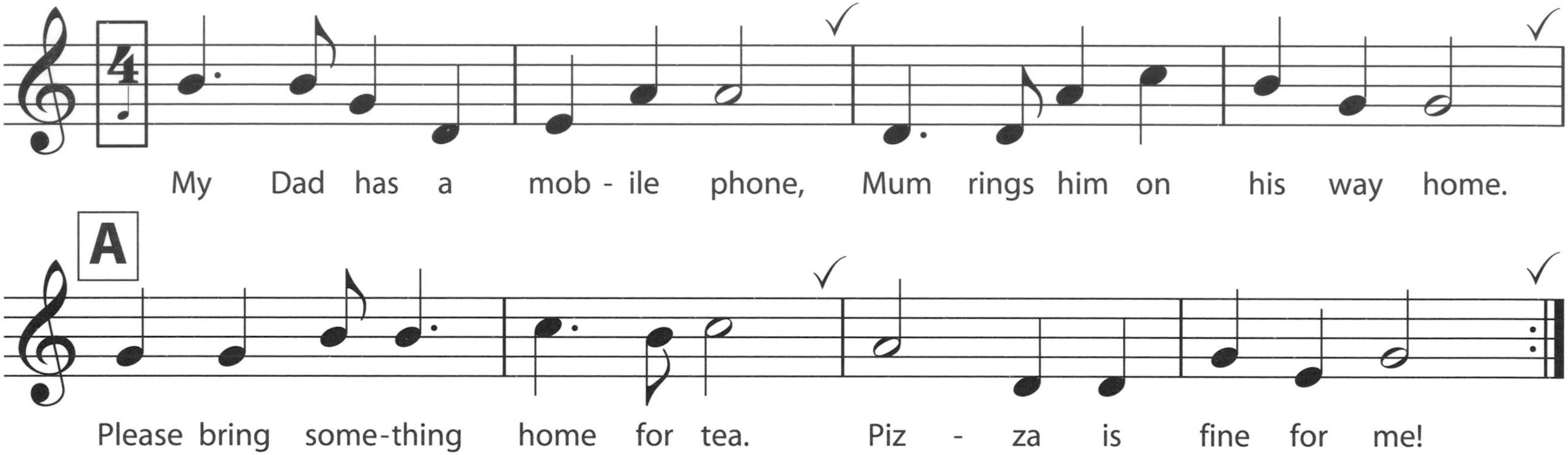

My Dad has a mob - ile phone, Mum rings him on his way home.

A

Please bring some-thing home for tea. Piz - za is fine for me!

Here is an **ostinato** (repeating pattern) for someone to play on xylophone.

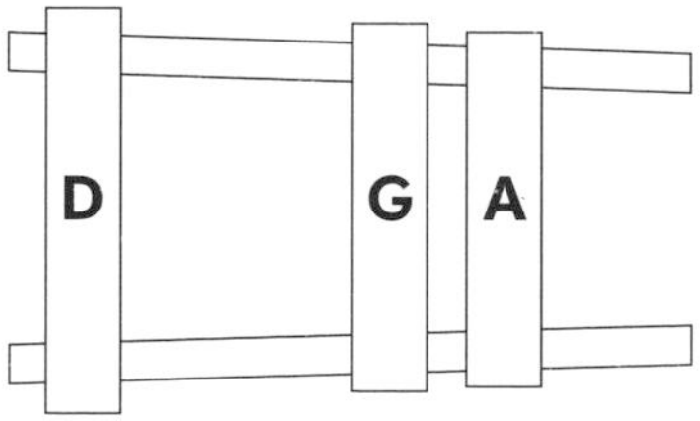

D   G   A

I like piz - za with some chips!

Lament

Notice that the tune begins on count 4.
Say 1–2–3 and begin to play on 4.
Later someone can add a rhythm **ostinato**.
Play it on claves or tambourine.

4
1 (2) (3) 4
1 (2) (3)

Fairly slowly

4
1 — (2) 3 4
1 — (2) — (3)
tut tu tut tu
1 — (2) and 3 4

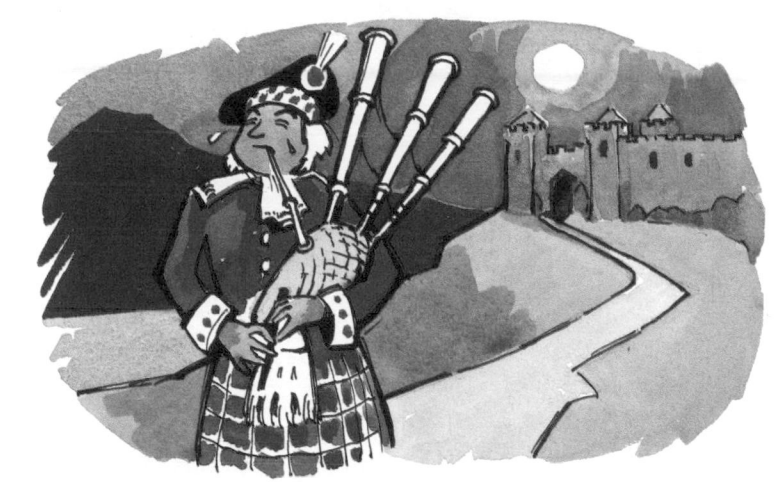

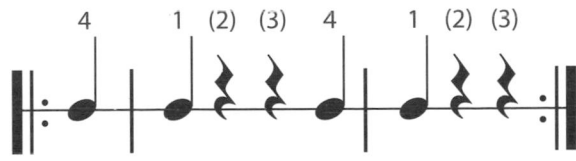

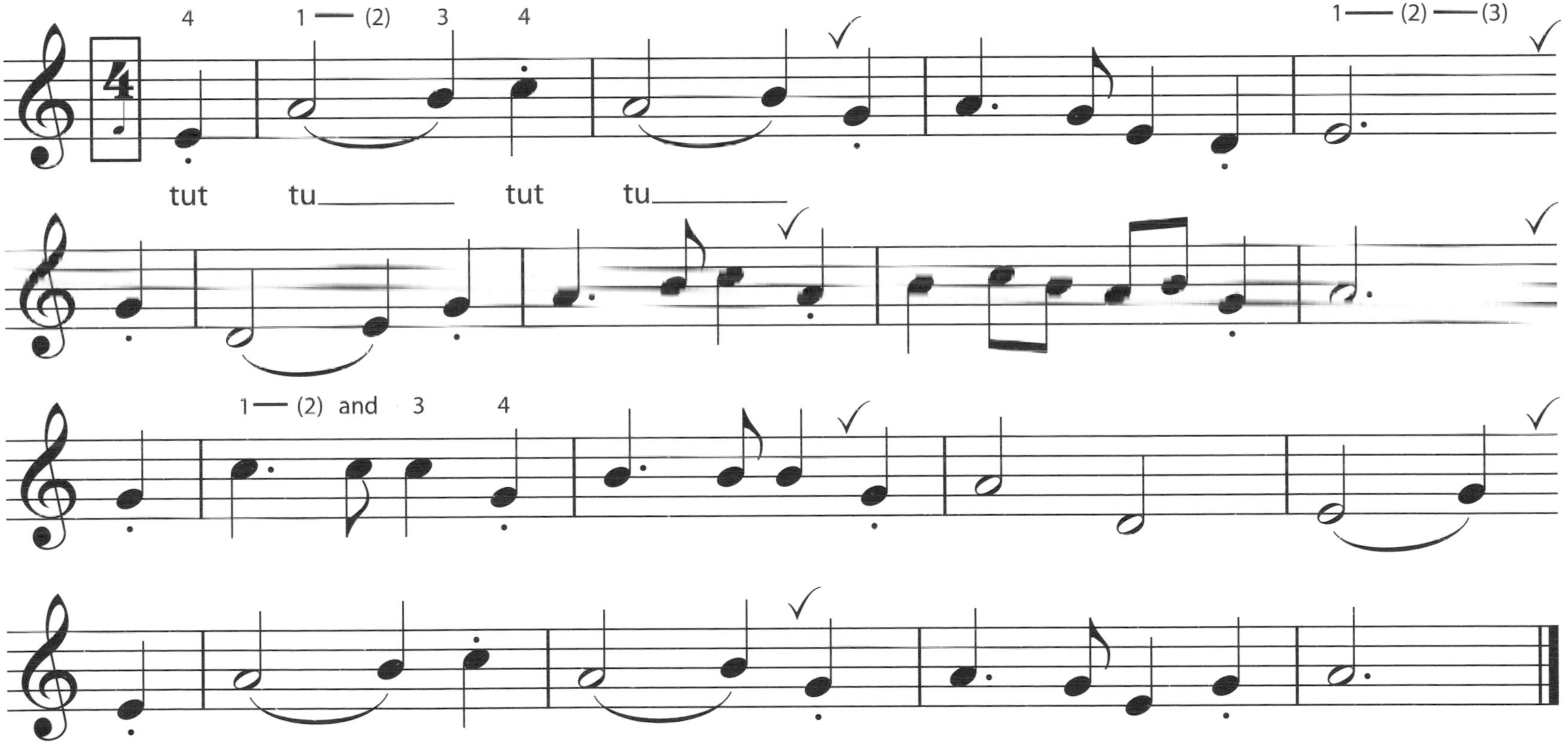

Copy-Cat Fanfare

The music for Group 2 copies Group 1. When this happens we call it a **canon**.

All learn Group 1 music first, then split into two groups.

Woody's Blues

Take care with the tied notes in bar 2.
In this tune the first two bars of music are used again.
Can you see where that is?

D.C. (Da Capo) means go back to the beginning and
repeat until **Fine** (End).

Fine

D.C. al Fine

43

Loch Morlich

When you can play this tune without mistakes, try the descant on the next page. Later, you and your friends could play both tunes at once.

Count 1–2–3 to help you to begin together.

Slowly, with a lilt

For more duets and other tunes using the notes and rhythms from this book, see *Recorder from the Beginning* **Tune Book 1.**

Descant to Loch Morlich

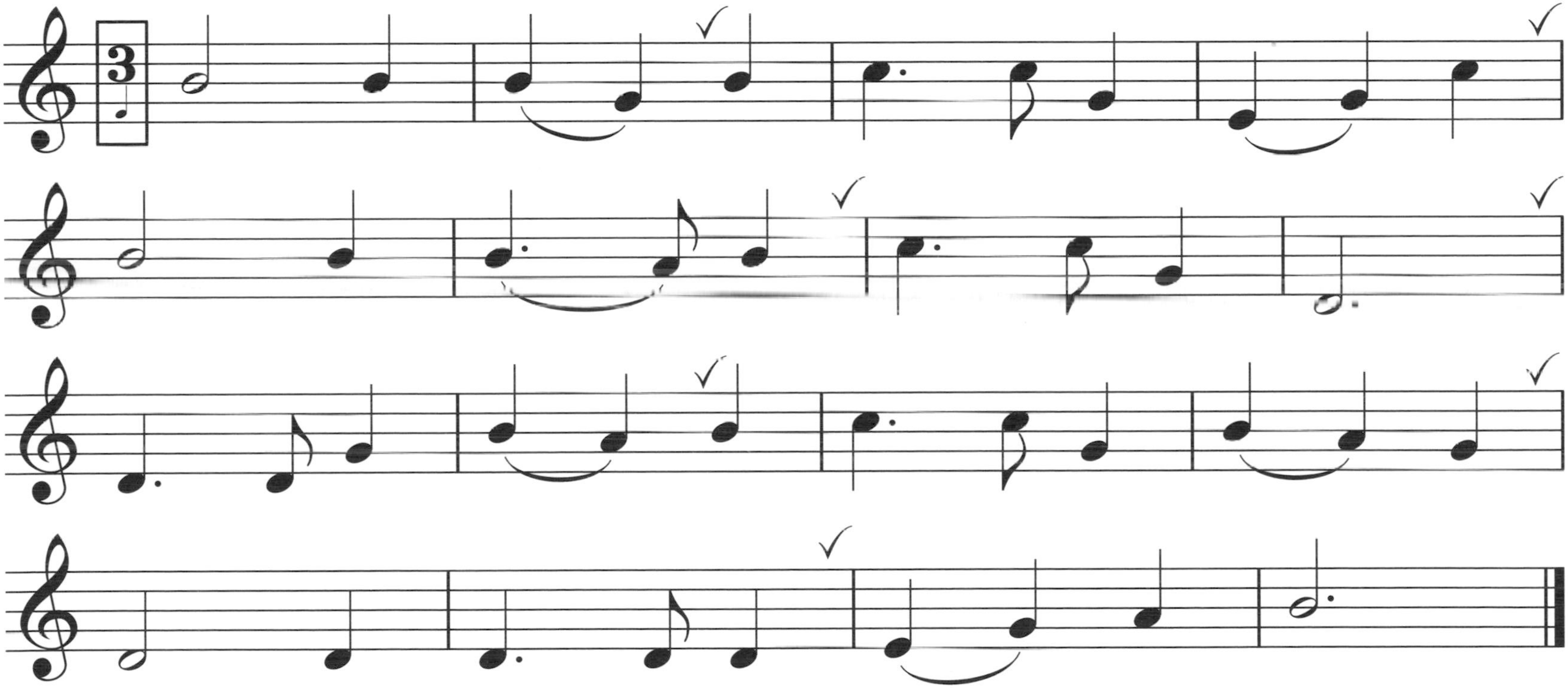

Making up tunes using notes we know

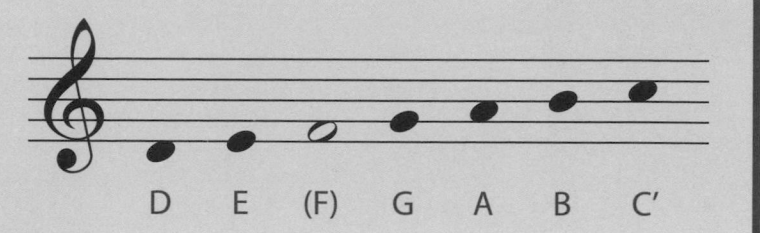

D E (F) G A B C'

For more tune writing see *Recorder from the Beginning* **Tune Book 1**.

A Say the words and clap the rhythm of **tune 1**. Then play it.

Tune 1 Saw A Flea

Saw a flea kick a tree, In the mid - dle of the sea.

Now say the words and clap the rhythm of **tune 2**.
Clap the rhythm of the first part again, saying the words quietly.

Tune 2 Saw A Crow

Saw a crow fly - ing low, Sev - 'ral miles be - neath the snow.

Make up a little tune on your recorder. Make it fit the words you clapped. Start with any note you choose. Try again, until you like your tune.

Play your tune, and finish it off with the rest of **tune 2**. You could write out the notes for your tune in pencil above the words.

B Make up an ending for **tune 3**. First play the beginning which is printed below. Now make up a tune to fit the rest of the words. Say the words and clap the rhythm to help you.

Tune 3 Saw A Bug

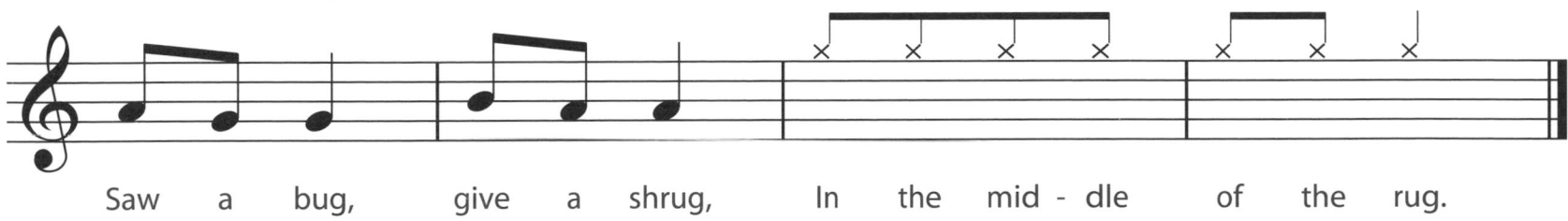

Saw　a　bug,　give　a　shrug,　In　the　mid - dle　of　the　rug.

Have some fun. Play the first part of **tune 3** with some friends. Choose one person to keep on playing and make up an ending. Then let someone else have a try. Write in the notes of the ending you like.

C See if you can make up all of **tune 4**. Use the words to give you the rhythm. You might need to write down the notes to help you remember your tune. Then you can play **tunes 4** and **5** straight after each other. Now can you play all the tunes without stopping?

Tune 4 Saw A Whale

Saw　a　whale　chase　a　snail,　All　a - round　a　wa - ter　pail.

Tune 5 Saw A Mule

Saw　a　mule　teach - ing　school,　To　some　bull - frogs　in　the　pool.